THE

CHRISTMAS
TRAIL GUIDE

25 DAYS OF ADVENT

NATHAN KING

For Mom and Dad.
You wrote Christmas on my heart.

THE ARRIVAL

What happens when you hear the word Christmas? I bet a cascade of nostalgic thoughts and feelings flood your heart and mind. If you're anything like me, it doesn't even take the word Christmas to queue the crescendo. Just the sound of a carol–and probably not even the entire thing. After only a few notes, your mind is probably off to the races. Christmas has been a big deal in many of our lives. Where does your memory take you when you ponder Christmas?

I think about my grandparents' house. Immediately I'm whisked away to Red Bench Road—to the tiny living room full of people I love, the humongous real Christmas tree my grandma always insisted on cramming in there, and the overwhelming pile of presents bulging out from under the tree. I think about the laughter, the smiles, the joyfulness of just being together. Many of my most powerful and vivid memories come from that room on that day–Christmas Eve.

I'm not sure why, but my family always celebrated together on the day before Christmas. And it has marked me. Forever. Because Christmas is not just something to be celebrated once a year. The beautiful legacy my family gave me was that Christmas is a celebration of anticipation.

It's way too easy these days to get lost in the commercialization of such a sacred moment. There are presents to be bought, decorations to hang, parties to attend, and ugly sweaters to find to wear to those parties. All of which is fun. But the fun was always meant to mark the phenomenal.

Christmas is an invasion. God invaded the pain of the world and our rebellion. He set a plan into motion to upend centuries of the status quo. Humankind had chosen its own way. God's kids were struggling. So God sent a child—His child—to fix it.

Christmas is about an innocent baby born into this world who would encounter all of the world's guilt. Christmas is about a King born into obscurity so you and I might become heirs to an eternal kingdom. Christmas is about one thing. Jesus came to us so that we would come to Him.

Getting caught up in the hustle and bustle of the holidays is easy. All of the fun things I mentioned earlier compete for our attention. But we can't afford to let the crazy win when it comes to Christmas. Don't ditch your fun holiday traditions, but do demand they kneel before the King of Christmas.

What's at stake for us is simple—a holy reminder. That's what I hope this book will be for you. A guide to help push back the societal demands of the holidays, even for only a few minutes a day. As you move through these pages, here is what will happen. You'll get back your perspective. You will appreciate the reason behind the season all the more. The hustle and bustle of all those parties and programs will crystallize in a beautiful memento, a foreshadowing of what we truly celebrate at Christmas. One of these pages will force you to face what Christmas has been to you. I hope it happens in the best possible way.

I wrote this book for one reason. Christmas is too important to lose to the chaos we've turned it into. If you feel that—I get it. I do too. Let me tell you a secret. I wrote this book for myself. Why? Because I needed a reminder. I know I can't afford to let Christmas become what our way of life sometimes demands it be. And I'm hoping together you and I can reclaim some of that childhood innocence we remember the most when we think of Christmas.

So, here's the plan. There are twenty-five written entries. Ideally, you could start on the first of December, and the readings will take you straight through to Christmas Day. Each entry has a Bible verse. I've done my best to explain the meaning behind the verse in a simple format I hope you can relate to. But each day also has a call to action. So here's your first one. You have to do more than just read this book. You have to *do* this book. If you only read it, well, I think it will still help you. But if you'll be brave enough to do this book, Christmas will become something new to you, or perhaps renewed.

Don't be intimidated. Don't be half-hearted, but also don't be hard on yourself. Just take five minutes every day to jump in and see where it takes you. You will not regret it. Your personal reason for the season is on the line here. And perhaps the way your kids or your loved ones look at Christmas is too.

Before we get started, let's get honest about something we both know will happen. Mr. Busy is going to show up big time. He rears his nasty humbug head pretty often this time of year. Don't give in. You have the same five minutes everyone else does. You just have to protect it. Is the heart of Christmas worth five minutes of your day for the next twenty-five days? Don't budge. I know you can do it if you want to.

So here we go. Here's what it really comes down to. Do you believe God would have you fully realize the joy, hope, love, and miracle of Christmas? I do! I believe it with everything I've got. And when we do, we'll embrace Christmas in a way that makes Buddy the Elf look like an amateur. We'll reorient our guiding focus around celebrating the most momentous moment in history–the day Jesus was born. The moment He became Emmanuel, God with us.

When you realize God is with you, it will change

more than Christmas. It will change everything. And, it will make all those parties and school plays a lot more fun. How? Because each and every one becomes another opportunity to celebrate the mission of Christmas. Jesus came to us so that we would come to Him. That, my friend, is certainly a trail worth traveling on together.

Merry Christmas.

PROMISED ONE

DAY 1

"A voice cries: 'In the wilderness prepare the way of the Lord; make straight in the desert a highway for our God. Every valley shall be lifted up, and every mountain and hill be made low; the uneven ground shall become level, and the rough places a plain. And the glory of the Lord shall be revealed, and all flesh shall see it together, for the mouth of the Lord has spoken.'" Isaiah 40:3–5 ESV

Twenty years ago, I met an old veteran. He started telling me about his time in the war. He described a big hole the soldiers would dig to hide in. He talked about bombers flying overhead to fight the Nazis nearby. He described how every night, the soldiers worried the bombs would fall on them.

One night he heard the familiar buzz of the bombers coming. The sky above him started lighting up with the sights of combat. Then explosions started happening above and in front of him. He crawled deep into a hole with his buddies, knowing the fight was out of their hands.

He said he prayed three prayers there that night. He prayed, "God save me," a salvation prayer. He called out for hope, "God help us!" And he prayed a prayer of promise, "God, I promise, if you get me out of here, I will be at church every time the doors are open." Every pastor I know would love that prayer. Want to guess where I met the old soldier? I met him at a church. He had kept his promise to God. God had kept his promise too. God had saved him.

I've never been in combat, but I bet it's easy to remember a promise you make in the middle of explosions. What about the everyday promises we make, though? I've promised to take out the trash. I've promised to watch movies with my kids. We promise our loved ones things all of the time. I've made lots of promises to God over the years too. I think most of us have.

Usually, we make promises to God when things are bad—or when we are in trouble. "God, help me get out of this jam, and I promise to serve you." "God, help my sister get well, and I promise to never lie again." Or, like the old soldier I told you about earlier, "God, get me out of here, and I'll never miss church again." I think the promises we make are so important. But, the promises God makes are even more important, which is what makes Christmas so amazing! It is a season to contemplate the promises of God.

God's promises all revolve around hope. Christmas is the celebration of hope invading our everyday world in the best way possible, JESUS. God wants to get into our lives. Why? Because you are somebody worth saving. We know this because of His promises to us.

God promised He was coming. In the days of Adam, God walked with him in the garden. In the days of Moses, the Holy Spirit led them through the wilderness. In the days of Isaiah, God promised He would be with them. This wasn't just a promise of solidarity or comfort. It was a declaration of intent. God was saying, "I will be with you."

What are you and I to do with that? We each have to make that decision. He comes to save us because He loves us. But we have to choose to accept it. Here's what happens when we do. Your valleys don't suddenly go away, but He lifts you up! Your mountains don't disappear, but He carries you through them! You don't stop experiencing trouble, but He keeps you steady. Life doesn't suddenly get easy, but He does give us peace. It's who He is. That is His promise. A promise of hope.

CHALLENGE: Write down one thing you can thank God for, just one. Now start telling God why you're thankful for it.

Day 2

"Today in the town of David a Savior has been born to you; he is the Messiah, the Lord." Luke 2:11 NIV

I remember as a young man watching my dad conduct business. All he needed was to exchange some words of promise and a handshake. That was it. The deal was sealed.

How much does a promise mean to you? I tell my oldest son all of the time, "All you have to give right now is your promise and your effort to keep it."

God had given His Word. He'd made a promise. In fact, scripture calls Jesus the "lamb slain before the foundations of the earth." In other words, before God said, "Let there be light," He whispered, "It is finished."

Those are all promises. Promises God kept. He gave

His Word. He kept His Word. Christmas is the birth of a Promise that predates the creation story. That is amazing.

Jesus is the Savior, the sent one. Heaven's invasion of our mess. Jesus is the Messiah, the Promised One. Heaven's guarantee things would be better. Jesus is our Lord. Heaven's High King.

You and I didn't do anything to deserve it, but we still get to participate. We are recipients. We are coheirs. Christmas is about your Savior, your Messiah, your Lord, showing up to flip the script on a world gone sideways.

I don't think it's an accident that one of the Gospel writers referred to Jesus as the Word. He is God's Promised One. Let that sink in. God promised and delivered.

I don't know about you, but I've made promises I haven't been able to keep. I don't make a habit out of it, but it happens. I don't try to do it on purpose. Instead, I just try to guard my promises, because I want my word to mean something. What I'm really guarding against is my own shortcomings.

God's promise carries no risk of falling short. His promise exceeds anything we can think, hope or imagine. Christmas is a promise worth looking forward to.

CHALLENGE: Take a minute to thank God for His promise to you. Now, take a moment to make yourself a promise—don't make it weird or complicated, just make it happen.

DAY 3

"This will be a sign to you: You will find a baby wrapped in cloths and lying in a manger." Luke 2:12 NIV

Have you ever tried to bargain with God? When I was young, I thought I could always negotiate with God. I didn't do it out of arrogance. I did it out of innocence. Because I learned God loved me at such a young age, I just assumed I could talk to Him the same way I talked to my friends. Spoiler alert: you can!

I really do believe God wants us to just tell Him what's on our hearts and minds. He is approachable. I also believe talking with God is a lot different than trading baseball cards with a buddy–especially when it comes to asking for a sign.

If you take a close look at scripture, it's the snobby guys who were always asking for a sign. They were the ones who acted like Jesus had something to prove. They failed to realize the signs had been hashed out in ages past. There were a lot of them.

Because my last name is King, I've always been drawn to stories about royalty. Seeing Jesus as a King comes easy to me. Maybe that's why it's so outstanding to me that the King of Heaven came to earth in such a humble way.

The shepherds were promised a sign. The coming king would not arrive to a never-ending parade of princes and kneeling dignitaries. He was to be born among the animals. He would be wrapped in humble clothes. His bassinet was to be a feeding trough. That was the sign.

Here's what I think this should teach us about Christmas. We need to look at it with new eyes. What if we put down our expectations? What if we let go of our assumptions? What if this year was about turning to Jesus with a humble heart, an open mind, and a willingness to bow our lives before the King who arrived in such humility?

Our response doesn't have to be complicated. Maybe all it means is instead of turning on the TV, what if we offered to take out the trash? If you always take out the trash, good for you. Do something different instead. Don't make love predictable; make it reliable. Then it will be both.

CHALLENGE: Do something kind for a friend or loved one.

Day 4

"The voice of one crying in the wilderness: 'Prepare the way of the Lord, make his paths straight,'" Mark 1:3 ESV

There aren't many wild places left in the world, but I am drawn to them. Hiking, hunting, and mountain biking are just some of the things I love to do outdoors. I find the wilderness compelling and refreshing. Maybe that's why John the Baptizer is one of my favorite people in the Bible.

John made a home out of the wild places. The outdoors were his sanctuary. The river was his altar, and the sky his painted glass. Choirs of crickets and birds chirped and buzzed a choral tune that stood in stark contrast to the hypocrisy John confronted.

John's message was clear, *"Get ready!"* He wanted everyone to know someone was coming. But it wasn't just anyone. It was *the Lord,* the one they had been waiting generations for. The Promised One. The Messiah.

As we ramp up to Christmas this year, what do the preparations look like for you? Have you already decorated? Is your shopping finished? No? Mine isn't either. As you prepare your home and your calendar, don't neglect your heart.

Our hearts are not unlike the wild places John preferred to dwell. I'd bet that doesn't surprise you. It shouldn't. God made them both. The problem with our heart is often the mess we make of it. We complicate things. If you want to untangle the mess, you have to make it simple again. You have to do what John said.

Prepare your heart for Christmas. Make sure there is room for Jesus. Nothing untangles our mess like inviting Jesus into it.

CHALLENGE: Put some time on your calendar every day for the next couple of weeks to do one thing: Prepare your heart for Jesus, the Lord of Christmas.

Day 5

"He will be great and will be called the Son of the Most High. The Lord God will give him the throne of his father David." Luke 1:32 NIV

Legacy is a powerful word. It encompasses the history of what came before you and what you leave behind. You are the pivotal moment in your legacy. What do you do with what came before? What will you leave behind?

Legacy is about promise. You were given your history. It was a gift. You had nothing to do with it—yet. I hope yours is a great history to look back on. Tragically, your legacy may be full of disaster and pain. For good or ill, you have an opportunity to embrace the promise of what came before. Either you will flourish and perhaps improve on what was passed down. Or you will depart the pain of those who missed the mark before you and press on toward something better you can leave behind for who comes next.

Christmas carries quite the legacy. Jesus was promised to be great. But He was born to a carpenter and his wife in a scandalous series of events. How could greatness come from that? He was promised to be the Son of the Most High, yet He showed up in the lowliest of places. Jesus was guaranteed a throne, yet He was killed on a cross. What do we do with that? We must embrace Christmas as what it is. It is a legacy.

Christmas is the turning point in the legacy of humanity. The pivotal moment in history. Where the promises of the past coalesced into the hopes for the future. Christmas is the invitation for us to take our place somewhere between *"Let there be light"* and *"Well done, good and faithful servant."*

What cherished Christmas traditions did you inherit that you hold onto? As I think about my family and how much has changed over the last couple of years, I've realized something incredible. My family is forging our Christmas Legacy. Here is what we all need to embrace. It's our promise to hold onto. Our promise to keep. Our promise to share with those who come after us.

CHALLENGE: Talk about a Christmas tradition with your family. Why do you do whatever it is? Or, start a new Christmas tradition today, but talk about why you are going to do it.

Day 6

"A shoot will come up from the stump of Jesse; from his roots a Branch will bear fruit." Isaiah 11:1 NIV

Every winter when I was a kid, my dad and I would walk into the woods and start cutting down trees. We would manhandle the logs, usually cedar, onto a trailer and sell them for extra money during the cold months when our watermelon farm wasn't producing fruit. I've seen hundreds of tree stumps. Thousands, really. Do you know what I've rarely seen? A new tree growing from an old stump.

The Prophet Isaiah spoke plainly. Though Jesse, the father of King David was dead, his heritage would live on. A new shoot would grow from an old stump. New life would sprout where things were thought long gone.

We live in a day when new things are often celebrated

for one reason: they are new. Just because a thing is new that doesn't make it better, it only makes it newer. How do we know if a new thing is a good thing? Simple. Look at its fruit. What is it producing in our world?

Christmas was about a new thing. The agreement Abraham had made with God was coming to a place of fulfillment. It was about to change in ways Abraham could never have imagined. The grace of Christmas spilling onto the scene shook loose old things and set off a chain reaction.

The legacy of what had been was deeply embedded in the culture of the people. Their traditions, laws, and even holidays revolved around it. They had deep roots.

Christmas changed things. But no one really knew it yet. As Jesus grew, the fruit of it became evident. He brought hope to people. He loved the overlooked and the downtrodden. He rejected the showy religion of man. He forestalled the fickle ambitions of politics. He even ignored the questions of the critics.

From the root of Jesse came the fruit of eternal love. Grace grew there. Hope blossomed. And nothing has ever been the same.

CHALLENGE: Examine your fruit. What is your life producing? Write it down on your phone or a notecard. If you don't like what you see—what can you do to change it?

Day 7

"Therefore the Lord himself will give you a sign. Behold, the virgin shall conceive and bear a son, and shall call his name Immanuel." Isaiah 7:14 ESV

There's a phrase we have all heard. I'd bet money we've not only heard it, but said it. What's the phrase? *"That is impossible."* See? It's familiar to us.

We both know a very simple truth: something said to be impossible is impossible for a reason. It cannot be done. Let me give you an example. It is impossible for me to grow wings and fly. I know. Of course this example sounds ludicrous. It sounds absurd because, by its very nature, it is impossible.

When God spoke through the Prophet Isaiah to declare a virgin would conceive a baby, it was absurd. Every parent knows there's only one thing that leads to babies. And by the very definition, a virgin cannot participate in the act that leads to creating a child. It is impossible. But like Jesus would go on to say later, "What is impossible with man is possible with God."

The virgin did conceive. Mary became pregnant with God's son. God did what cannot be done in order to initiate what you and I could never do. We could never deal with our own sin. That would be impossible. Just like a dead man could never live again. But God did all of that.

The virgin birth was a cosmic declaration. *Take note. Things are different now. What you knew as possible has been forever changed.* God did it. God moved the paradigm of what was possible in order to be with you. He loves you that much.

Every time we celebrate Christmas, we are cheering for the moment the impossible became possible. The star on your tree isn't just a pretty light. It's a reflection of the spark of hope the virgin birth ignited across history.

If something seems impossible this Christmas season, close your eyes, open your heart, and declare, *"God, nothing is impossible with you."*

CHALLENGE: *Every time you turn on a light today, repeat this prayer, "God, nothing is impossible with you."*

FAMILY CHAT

What did you learn about Christmas this week?

What promise from God means the most to you?

Which challenge was the hardest? Which one was easy?

How is God drawing you closer to Him right now?

Where did you need help from someone?

Where did you help someone else?

Do you feel like Christmas means more to you today? How?

What are you looking forward to most this Christmas?

CHRISTMAS JOURNAL

_____

_____

_____

_____

_____

_____

_____

_____

GIFT OF GOD

DAY 8

"While they were there, the time came for her to give birth. She gave birth to a son, her firstborn. She wrapped him in a blanket and laid him in a manger, because there was no room in the hostel." Luke 2:6-7 MSG

Jesus didn't magically appear. He was born. Just like you were. Well, maybe not just like you. I think they were fresh out of epidurals and birthing rooms in Bethlehem.

As a father of four, I often find myself thinking about Joseph. What was going through his mind as the Son of God was about to be born into his family? Mary gets a lot of attention, and for good reason. But as a father, I can't help but imagine the weight Joseph must have felt. The journey they took to arrive at Bethlehem couldn't have been easy. It wasn't normal for people to travel long distances back then, but he did it.

I watched in awe as all four of my kids came into this world, but I wasn't surprised about how they got here. I knew the part I played to make it happen. Okay, I know that's awkward—let's move on. Joseph witnessed the birth of the Son of God. A birth conceived by the Spirit of God. A birth foretold to him by a Guardian of Heaven.

On the night of my daughter's due date, I was sitting on the couch playing video games with my friends, waiting for my wife to give the word. I'd been anticipating her declaration all day. Finally, shortly after midnight, it came. She walked into the living room and declared, like the old monkey from *The Lion King*, "It is time." I'd been waiting all day, and it still took too long to hit me. It was time.

What did Joseph do when the time came? Well, we know, don't we? He tried to get a room for his wife, but he couldn't because all the travelers had taken all the spare rooms. So the King of Kings was born to the traveling carpenter and placed in a manger. At least they had a blanket.

Christmas is the story of an upside-down kingdom. The King of Glory coming in humility. Want to move closer to the heart of Christmas? Pursue humility. This doesn't mean thinking less of yourself—it means rising to the fullness of who you are and submitting yourself to the goodness of God's plan for you, just like Joseph did.

. . .

CHALLENGE: What is one thing you can do to serve someone in your life today? Do it. Go above and beyond what is required in order to really make it special for them.

Day 9

"But Mary treasured up all these things, pondering them in her heart." Luke 2:19 ESV

One day, as I worked in the garage, one of my sons approached me glowing. "Daddy, I found something," he beamed as he exclaimed.

"What is it, buddy?" I asked him in return. I will never forget his sweet innocent answer.

"I found a treasure," he declared, sticking out his dirty little hand. He unfurled his fingers to reveal a shiny plastic bauble he'd uncovered in the dirt behind our house.

"Wow! You sure did. How cool!" And before he returned to playing, I encouraged him to keep it somewhere safe because it was important to him.

A few days later, I was working back in the garage again when he came to me downtrodden. He had lost his treasure. As I talked with him about it, it became clear, he had not kept it safe. He had been too busy playing.

I love the language Luke used to describe Mary's response to the birth of Jesus. She had been trusted with the greatest treasure in all of human history. She responded accordingly. She treasured what was happening. How could she not?

Mary wasn't chosen at random. Something about her drew the heart of God in her direction. Mary would treasure the baby Messiah and care for him. God treasured Mary. Mary and Joseph would keep baby Jesus safe. God would protect them. The lesson is simple. You care *for* what you care *about*.

What do you care about? What do you care for? Take a look at your actions over the course of the past week, month, year. Where did you aim your effort?

Mary's actions certainly declared her affection and intentions toward the baby King of Kings, but it did not end there. She pondered them in her heart. Typically we would think of pondering as something done in our head. It's the act of thinking about something. But Mary was Jesus' mom. She got out of her head and went all heart when it came to treasuring Christmas. What if we didn't overthink Christmas this year? What if we let our hearts lead us toward what we treasure most?

. . .

CHALLENGE: What is your favorite Christmas moment? What do you treasure about Christmas? How can you put your whole heart into it this year? Text a friend and tell them what you plan to do.

Day 10

"Every good and perfect gift is from above, coming down from the Father of the heavenly lights, who does not change like shifting shadows." James 1:17 NIV

What is the worst Christmas gift you have ever received? Be honest. I'd bet money it was an article of clothing or a fruitcake. Do people really eat those?

When I was growing up, one of my aunts always made us fake brand-name clothing for Christmas. As a kid, that was horrifying. I was never very trendy, but that didn't mean I wanted to run around in blatant knockoffs while the other kids sported their flashy new clothes.

It's funny how much perspective can shift over time. No, I don't want any knockoff clothing now either, but I am able to see the heart behind the gift. I can see the perfect purity of the motive. I totally get it.

I might have shifted in my perspective over the years when it comes to what makes a good gift, but God never has. God is steady. He is stable.

I love the language James used to describe God. He does not change. He does not shift around like the shadows. The remarkable nature of this statement really comes home when you take into account the truth about Jesus. Jesus is repeatedly described as the Light of the World. But growing up, I bet James just saw Him as his older brother.

To James, Jesus wasn't the Messiah. He was just the perfect brother who was impossible to live up to. I bet it wasn't until much later–when James thought about Jesus, that it all made sense for him.

How has Christmas changed for you over the years? Maybe some family has passed away and your traditions have shifted. Mine have. We usually don't know what we have until we no longer have it.

What if our next step toward the heart of Christmas was a step of appreciation? Let's get really intentional about telling the people in our life how much they mean to us this year. Why? Because it's the people in our life who are the real gift.

CHALLENGE: Tell two people in your life what they mean to you today.

Day 11

"And this is the testimony: God has given us eternal life, and this life is in his Son." 1 John 5:11 NIV

I meet a lot of people. In fact, it's no exaggeration to say I've met thousands of people. As a new relationship is forming, one of my favorite things to do is to sit down with someone over a meal. I want to learn about them and fellowship with them.

My favorite part of meeting people has always been getting to learn their story. What brought them into my life? Why did they choose to show up at my church? What is their history? I ask a lot of questions.

Everyone has an important story to tell because everyone is living an important story. When I was growing up in church, we called these stories a testimony. A testimony is just a fancy way of naming your story. It's a way to intentionally frame the story God is telling through your life.

God has a story too. It isn't just *His* testimony. It is *the* testimony. Christmas is the culmination of it. What is God's testimony? *"God has given us eternal life..."*

I don't think anyone breathing can properly understand the scope of eternal life. We talk a lot about it. We may even dream about it. We certainly hope where eternal life is concerned, but I'm convinced the concept of eternity is beyond our ability to comprehend in this life. Life without limitations is God's story. He made a gift of it, for you and for me, and everyone we care about.

God's gift of eternal life is clear, *"... and this life is in his Son."* Jesus brought the gift of eternal life to mankind. The Christmas baby would grow up to give up His life willingly for you and me. He would give His life away. That's also part of God's story.

The gift of eternal life arrived in Bethlehem under a bright starry sky to the angel choirs, the heralding of prophets past and wise men to come. Shepherds came to pay homage to the Lamb of God. And in the middle of all of this, in the midst of God's story, God knew it would be your story too, someday. Because Jesus came to you so that you could come to Him.

CHALLENGE: *Ask someone to tell you their story today. If you have time, tell them yours.*

DAY 12

"This is how much God loved the world: He gave his Son, his one and only Son. And this is why: so that no one need be destroyed; by believing in him, anyone can have a whole and lasting life." John 3:16 MSG

I have four kids. And you can't have any of them. I know. That's a ridiculous thing to say. Who is going to give their kid away? I'm not. Neither are you. But God did. And He did it—FOR YOU.

Can you imagine a love so outlandish and incomprehensible it would compel you to give your son away? It is so beyond my ability to comprehend it gives me a headache if I think about it too much.

The gift of Christmas is the gift of ultimate love. God gave His only begotten son. But it wasn't without purpose. It wasn't divine virtue signaling. It was pointed and purposeful. The intent was clear. There was a history behind the moment marked by the intended change.

Jesus was born. Jesus came to us. So we would come to Him. Because belief in Jesus is the fork in the road. Christmas was the moment that presented an opportunity before all humanity.

I've always found it interesting that King Herod had issued a decree to have all the baby boys in the region murdered. But it's beyond interesting. It is villainous. It was a coward's move perpetrated by someone who should have known better. Because evil can't win over love. Evil tried to take out God's gift before the gift could be realized. All because someone wanted to choose their kingdom over God's kingdom.

A choice is before us. We stand at the Crossroads of Christmas. Do we choose Jesus and life? Or do we ignore the gift in pursuit of our own kingdom. The thing about a gift is that it cannot be taken. It can only be given. It can only be received. Any other interaction is an affront to the intended gift.

Our choice is really about love. What do we love more? Do we love our kingdom or do we love *the kingdom*?

CHALLENGE: *Today, do something entirely selfless for someone you love.*

Day 13

"In everything I did, I showed you that by this kind of hard work we must help the weak, remembering the words the Lord Jesus himself said: 'It is more blessed to give than to receive.'" Acts 20:35

A couple of years ago, I turned forty. My loved ones celebrated. It was a great day as the calls and texts poured in. I had concocted a plan earlier in the day, so that afternoon, after we picked up the kids from school, my wife and I drove across town to a store. I told the kids they were going in to help me pick out my birthday present.

When we got to the front of the store, I spilled the beans. I told them that, instead of getting myself something for my birthday, I wanted to get them all a gift for my birthday. You can imagine how excited they were. My wife got a new watch. My kids all picked out a toy. And I received the gift of giving on my big day. It was great.

As I have gotten older, I love giving gifts so much more than getting one. But, it has taken me eighteen years to be able to wait until Christmas to give Jamie her present. With my kids, it is so much worse!

Each year at Christmas, I realize how incredibly blessed I am. Sure, it's fun when your loved ones honor you with a memorable gift. But I'm realizing more and more that I don't need it anymore. What I actually need is for my heart to be more like the heart of Jesus. I need to lean toward giving.

Do you know what's going on in your brain when you give? It's pretty incredible. You actually love the person you gave to even more when your motives are pure. Imagine that. No wonder Christmas is so full of joy and good cheer.

Here's the new lens I'm hoping we'll look at Christmas through this year: Let's see what we can give instead of what we can get.

Jesus came with one simple mission. To give. But He was going big. He was giving Himself. His plan was to give His very life. Imagine how much He must love you to do that.

CHALLENGE: Give something away today. Don't overthink it. Just do it.

DAY 14

"Thanks be to God for his indescribable gift!" 2 *Corinthians 9:15 NIV*

Who is the talker in your family? The one that never shuts up. You probably have one. I have a few in mine. I have bad news for you, if you can't think of one, you are the talker in your family. People with the gift of gab have no trouble running their mouths. I should know. I am one. Words come pretty easy to folks like us.

There is one set of words I'm trying to be better at saying. Especially to the people I really hope will hear them. What are the words? *Thank you.* I'm trying to be more intentional with my gratitude. Recently I was given a powerful reminder of the importance of gratitude.

A few days ago at church, a friend of mine walked up and put something in my hand. Then he said something bizarre to me. He said, "Tango Yankee." At first, I thought I'd misunderstood because it was early in the morning. But when I looked at what was in my hand, I saw a black and white poker chip with the words "Tango Yankee" inscribed. My friend explained that Tango Yankee is military lingo for Thank You. It's like a code they use over the radio to express gratitude for something. But my friend wasn't finished. He looked me in the eyes and said, "what you do in this life matters." It was touching.

How often does gratitude get the final say at Christmas? My grandpa was always so tender-hearted at Christmas. He would become visibly emotional because of how our family showed their love and appreciation for him. I feel like I can still hear his *"Thank you"* ringing in my ears. I hope even more than that I can share it with my family and friends.

When we get gratitude right, it's our way of looking the one we're thankful for in the eye and declaring, "What you do in this life matters." That's no small thing to declare. As people of faith, we should be pretty quick to declare it. Why? Because of God's gift to you. His son.

There have been more books written about Jesus than any other subject in the history of humanity. We'll never run out of words where Jesus is concerned. Because we can never stop describing the indescribable gift of God. But I can think of two words that are a great start: Thank you.

. . .

CHALLENGE: Find someone you interact with on a regular basis in a seemingly small way. It could be the barista at your favorite coffee shop or the teacher who watches your kids in the pick up line. Tell them your version of this: "Thank you for what you do. It means a lot to me."

FAMILY CHAT

What did you learn about Christmas this week?

What gift from God means the most to you?

Which challenge was the hardest? Which one was easy?

How is God drawing you closer to Him right now?

Where did you need help from someone?

Where did you help someone else?

Do you feel like Christmas means more to you today? How?

What are you looking forward to most this Christmas?

CHRISTMAS JOURNAL

_____

_____

_____

_____

_____

_____

_____

_____

_____

IMPOSSIBLE LIGHT

DAY 15

"In him was life, and that life was the light of all mankind. The light shines in the darkness, and the darkness has not overcome it." John 1:4-5 NIV

As I sit and write this, it is my favorite time of year. I don't like the cold, but a lot of things I love come around when it's cold outside. For example, I love Arkansas Razorback basketball–and basketball season just started. I love deer hunting with my dad. We went several days this past week. I love the Holidays. Thanksgiving is this week. Christmas is just around the corner. I enjoy each of those things a lot, even though I don't like the cold.

As much as I love this season, it's important to understand there are many people who struggle this time of year. The holidays are hard for them because of things they have gone through. This season may not feel like a blessing; it may seem like a burden. It may feel overcast instead of like an opportunity.

Do you ever feel like you're living under a shadow? I think we all go through those kinds of seasons. Whether this describes you or not, it is important for us to understand the truth.

Darkness is not winning. Not now. Not ever. Not in your life. Not in your family. Not in your business. Not in your marriage. Darkness has not blotted out God's promise for you. Darkness has not overshadowed God's purpose for you. Darkness has not overcome the Light.

Maybe there have been more than a few things throwing shade on this season of your life. Whether doubt snuck up on you or rolled in like a loud summer storm, I want you to know the Light of God is shining on you.

This is going to sound silly to you, but do you know what the best way to get out of the shade is? It's obvious isn't it? Step into the light.

Every day I have to recharge my batteries. I need to get outside. Sometimes I just walk laps around our building. I need to be in the light. We all do.

Not that you need my permission, but you may need an idea. If life has been a little dark lately, get outside of wherever you've been struggling. Maybe it will be as easy as taking a walk. It might mean you need a vacation. Somebody will read this and realize they actually need to change addresses. Don't wait. Don't put it off. Just move from the place in your life where darkness is trying to keep tabs on you and get into the light.

CHALLENGE: Take a walk today. Get out into the light. As you walk, talk to God about the things bothering you.

DAY 16

"And again, Isaiah says, 'The Root of Jesse will spring up, one who will arise to rule over the nations; in him the Gentiles will hope.' May the God of hope fill you with all joy and peace as you trust in him, so that you may overflow with hope by the power of the Holy Spirit." Romans 15:12-13 NIV

I recently heard a friend say, "you can live three weeks without food, you can live three days without water, but you can't live three seconds without hope." I think one of the greatest tragedies of our lifetime is the wholesale abandonment of hope by so many.

One of my favorite authors was doing an interview recently when he said something that caught my attention, "Hope is not a plan of action." While I would agree with his sentiment, I think his thought is incomplete.

Because *real* hope is not about *not* doing anything. It's not pie in the sky. Real hope is about real trust. Hope may not be a plan of action, but real hope is about planning to act.

Christmas is the advent of hope. One worth putting your hope in showed up. Our hope is rooted in God's actions. Apparently, hope is a team sport. Joy and peace show up too. And those Gentiles Isaiah talked about? Well, unless you're Jewish, that's you.

Christmas is an opportunity to find the hope that fuels you. The side effect is the runoff that spills all around you. Your hope becomes the hope of everyone it touches. When hope becomes real to you, hope becomes contagious. Moving toward Jesus means moving toward hope. It's an intentional shift in your heart's posture. It's a big adjustment to your attitude.

Hope and pessimism are incompatible. Don't reject reality. Don't bury your head in the sand and wish for a magic rescue. That will just make you one of those weird Christians people write off. Instead, look reality in the face, dare not to be intimidated, and trust in a really good God. The God of hope.

CHALLENGE: Write something you've been worried about on a piece of paper. Pray this prayer as you tear the paper into little pieces, "God, I don't know what's going to happen. But I do know I am going to trust in you."

DAY 17

"When they saw the star, they were overjoyed." Matthew 2:10 NIV

A few months ago, my family was hiking at one of our favorite spots. At the end of the hike was a cave. The unique opportunity in this particular cave was a waterfall that waited inside. So, all six of us scrambled into the cave to reach the hidden beauty in the darkness. A little way into the cave something happened. My wife was gripped by terrible anxiety. This was completely out of character for her, so it couldn't be ignored. She decided to head back for the beginning. Among the twists and turns of the passage she only felt her anxiety deepen. Until at last she caught a glimpse of light. The weight of her anxiousness gave way to the joy of the light.

For centuries the Hebrew people had been awaiting the Messiah. They struggled through wicked kings, subjugation at the hands of tyrants, and exile from the Promised Land. Even in the era leading to the arrival of Jesus, they were being crushed beneath the cruel occupation of Roman might.

Jesus is the light of the world—born into darkness. The wise men who sought the Promised One looked for the signs from within the darkness. And they saw it.

Imagine centuries of expectation merging with a singular moment. A sign. A star in the sky.

When you were growing up, was there a gift you were really anxious to get? Do you remember what it was like to greatly anticipate receiving something you'd been waiting a long time for?

Now, imagine what it would be like if you had been waiting your entire life for an event to happen. But, what if it was an event generations of your people had been anticipating? That's exactly what those who were anticipating the Messiah experienced with Jesus.

Their response was probably not much different than yours when you discovered your long-awaited gift. They were full of joy. They were so full of joy it overflowed. What if we were so full of joy this Christmas, it spilled over? Imagine what it would be like to be the one radiating joy this Christmas.

CHALLENGE: Listen to the classic Christmas carol "Joy to the World." Make it more than a song today, make it your prayer.

DAY 18

"The next day John saw Jesus coming toward him and said, 'Look! The Lamb of God who takes away the sin of the world!'" John 1:29 NLT

Have you ever been mistaken for someone else? It used to happen to me all the time. In fact, the basketball coach I played under for years routinely called me by my cousin's name. These days Christmas has a bit of an identity crisis. It's no wonder so many people in our world are confused about things. We can't even agree on Christmas.

John the Baptizer wasn't confused about Christmas. He knew what it was all about. When people at a place called Bethany confused him for the promised Messiah, he quickly corrected them—and then this happened: John saw Jesus coming.

The beauty of the moment was sealed by the hope all of us have a chance to embrace at Christmas. John saw Jesus coming, but why? Because he was expecting Jesus to show up. He was living life expecting Jesus to be there. When you know why Jesus came, you can anticipate where He will be. He came to be *with* us—so let's expect Him to show up. Even better, what if we assumed He was always right there *with* us. Let's live our life expecting Jesus to be there.

Jesus was moving toward John. Have you ever considered this? Jesus is moving to you. He isn't moving away from you. Why did He walk toward John? Simple. He loved John. Guess what? Jesus loves you. Christmas came for you.

John wasn't surprised, but he was still in awe. He told everyone to look. Why did he do that? Because Jesus is worth paying attention to. Are we giving Him our attention? If we believe He is always with us, how does that affect the way we move through our day?

A long time ago, lambs were sacrificed as part of a covenant between God and men. As John pointed out that day on the riverbank, Jesus is the Lamb of God. He became the ultimate sacrifice.

Not a lamb of men. A lamb given by God. The babe in the manger didn't stay a baby because He came to confront our sin. To overcome it. To take away the sin of the world. Where does He take it?

As far as the East is from the West. Because He loves you.

. . .

CHALLENGE: Turn toward the rising sun and tell God, "Thank You for your Perfect Lamb. Thank You for your Son. Thank You for taking away my sin."

DAY 19

"An angel of the Lord appeared to them, and the glory of the Lord shone around them, and they were terrified. But the angel said to them, 'Do not be afraid. I bring you good news that will cause great joy for all the people.'" Luke 2:9-10 NIV

Can I be really honest? If someone came up to me today and started telling me about the time angels showed up and spoke to them, I would start thinking they need to see a really good therapist. It's not that I don't believe in angels. It's just that conversations with angels aren't the norm where I'm from.

What if an angel did show up? I bet my reaction wouldn't be very different from the shepherds. Your reaction probably wouldn't be so different, either.

What's amazing about Luke's story is that it wasn't *only* the angels the shepherds were reacting to. It was the glory of the Lord they responded to, "And they were terrified." That seems like the proper response.

It should be reassuring to both of us that the story doesn't end with the shepherds being afraid. In fact, the charge leveled their way was, "Do not be afraid." Of course, if you're thinking what I'm thinking, you're thinking, "Easier said than done."

The change agent where the shepherds' fear was concerned wasn't merely an angelic command. No, it was angelic encouragement. What was the encouragement? A simple promise. The angels declared the promise of God had at last arrived. The good news of the Gospel was becoming reality. And the result was a change of disposition. Fear was out. Joy was in. What began with the fear of a few (the shepherds) was about to be joy for everyone. Joy is cool like that.

Maybe your life has been full of fear recently. Flip the script. Get joy in on it. I get it. It is easier said than done, but that doesn't mean it's not worth doing. The shepherds were gripped by fear when they were standing in the middle of it. But when the promised good news reached their ears, they traded up for joy. This Christmas, resolve to set aside a fear you've been keeping around. Trade up for joy.

. . .

CHALLENGE: Write your fear on a small piece of paper. Give it to a friend or family member and ask them if they will pray for you to have joy instead.

DAY 20

"The one who is the true light, who gives light to everyone, was coming into the world. He came into the very world he created, but the world didn't recognize him." John 1:9-10 NLT

I like to go outside every once in a while and just stand in the sunlight. I don't usually stand there very long. Most of the time, it's just about half a minute. When I do, I close my eyes, lift my chin a bit, and let the sun shine on my face. It's invigorating.

What would happen if you and I both walked out into the sunlight at the same time? We would both be in the light. That's pretty straightforward, right? The sun is there for everybody. You don't need any special privileges to experience the sun. You only need to get outside.

Jesus is the Son of God, the Light of the World, or as John stated, "the True Light." You don't need any special privileges to experience Jesus. You just declare in your heart you want to move toward Him. When you do, something beautiful happens, you discover that Immanuel (God with us) was already right there waiting for you.

The first Christmas was a moment of cosmic significance. The Son showed up for everybody. The True Light arrived to peel back the darkness, but not everyone understood what was happening. Can you imagine waiting for someone for generations only to miss them entirely when they finally showed up? What a tragedy.

Make this Christmas one where you take the time to stand before the Son. Get still before Him, even if only for a moment. As you do, reflect on your life. Reflect on the opportunities you've had to be like Jesus. Did you love your neighbor? Did you love your enemy? What did you do?

Recognizing Christmas for what it really is means moving past the stuff we sometimes turn it into. The fun stuff is fun for a reason. I'm not saying you need to put all that aside and become Mr. Scrooge. I am saying be honest about what Christmas is. You owe it to yourself to take a look at your Christmas and see if you recognize Jesus in it.

. . .

CHALLENGE: What holy tradition can you add to your Christmas celebration this year? Reading the Christmas story? Setting up a nativity? Maybe you already do that. When you do, take a moment to pray and reflect. Look for Jesus in the moment.

Day 21

"Seeing was believing. They told everyone they met what the angels had said about this child. All who heard the shepherds were impressed." Luke 2:17-18 MSG

Has anyone ever told you something you just knew couldn't be true? If you grew up with a sibling, this probably happened to you. Or, if you have young kids, you've experienced it too. I can almost decide by the tone of their voice if my kids are blowing sunshine, or if they are telling the truth. It's like a superpower for dads.

Do you think everyone believed the shepherds when they went about proclaiming all the incredible things the angels had shared with them? Actually, we don't know. We do know they were impressed. But you can be impressed at the sheer audacity of a lie someone tries to get you to believe.

If my kids come to me with a story they know isn't true, I can detect the fiction because of their clear disbelief in their own story. The shepherds believed and for good reason. They had holy proof. They experienced angelic admonition. And then they saw the truth with their own eyes. Seeing is believing.

Obviously you and I don't have a time machine. We can't go check out the baby Jesus lying in a manger for ourselves. As far as I know, heaven hasn't started a YouTube channel where we can catch the highlights of holy history. But what we can do is believe. We can trust. And we can come to Christmas in a way that helps others believe.

What if your belief was all it took to help your struggling friend find hope this Christmas? No pressure. In all seriousness, we wield something powerful when we believe. Don't make it an attempt to impress anyone with your proclamations. If you want applause, join the circus. If you want to make a difference in the lives of the ones close to you—believe. Simply believe. And let the radiance of your trust in what God did on the first Christmas make the difference around you.

CHALLENGE: Tell someone what you believe Christmas is all about.

Family Chat

What did you learn about Christmas this week?

What impossible thing has God done in your life?

Which challenge was the hardest? Which one was easy?

How is God drawing you closer to Him right now?

Where did you need help from someone?

Where did you help someone else?

Do you feel like Christmas means more to you today? How?

What are you looking forward to most this Christmas?

CHRISTMAS JOURNAL

_____

_____

_____

_____

_____

_____

_____

_____

_____

KING OF KINGS

DAY 22

"So they hurried off and found Mary and Joseph, and the baby, who was lying in the manger." Luke 2:16 NIV

Raise your hand if you're impatient. I'm half kidding. If you're as impatient as I am, you don't want to waste any time raising your hand. I am painfully impatient sometimes. I often feel like I'm headed somewhere in a hurry. The biggest issue with living life in a hurry is that your life will just fly by.

What God is teaching me as I get older is that it's okay to move a little slower sometimes. There are times to move slow and times to move fast. These days I prefer to only get in a hurry when I'm moving toward something to be excited about.

At the Dawn of Christmas the shepherds encountered the miraculous as they kept vigil in the fields. An angel choir heralded the arrival of King Jesus. The shepherds didn't waste any time. They hurried off. They moved with purpose—toward Jesus.

The hustle and bustle of the holidays can be taxing, but if we're being honest, it's not *only* the holidays that seem hectic. Life gets hectic too. What if we learned something from the shepherds?

Let's make a decision this year to be where we are. To keep a vigil over what God made us stewards of. Let's watch and wait–at least until the call comes in. Once it does, let's move with haste. We should hurry off when we're moving toward the King of Christmas. We should hurry off when we're moving toward Jesus.

The shepherds didn't stop being shepherds because they had seen the baby Messiah. I bet they went right back to their fields and their flock. But it wasn't the same anymore. Every night sky became a reminder of the time the angels declared the glory of God. Every baby lamb became a moment to realize the reality of the Lamb of God.

What if we took two steps closer to what God wanted for us today? We're in a hurry, right? First, let's look around at where we are and take note of what reminds us of God's goodness in our life. Second, only get in a hurry when you move toward something you are excited about.

. . .

CHALLENGE: Move a bit slower through your day—especially where people you love are concerned. Unless, of course, you're trying to get home to them. Then, go ahead, hurry off.

DAY 23

"Glory to God in the highest heaven, and on earth peace to those on whom his favor rests." Luke 2:14 NIV

My grandpa was known for a lot of things. He was a happy, hardworking man with an optimistic outlook on life. Anytime something good would happen, he was known to dance a little country jig and shout two words, "WELL, GLORY!"

Grandpa's declaration wasn't much different from the angels' that wild night in the fields near Bethlehem. He knew where the glory goes. God gets the credit. God gets the glory. Whatever worship we can muster, we aim His way. It is His glory.

As amazing as God's glory is, the angels had more to declare. The Heavenly Host let loose a torrent like a mighty angel band booming a proclamation of worship for the birth of the baby Messiah. They esteemed Him in worship and heaped on adoration. Also, they declared peace had made landfall. The peace came with a package deal. It was both peace and favor.

In the moment of the angels' declaration, it was a promise of favor for the shepherds. It was an act of reassurance. And it was a beacon of hope. They had the details already. A Savior had been born. They had a promise. Glory, peace, and favor had arrived too.

Their Christmas journey was no different than ours. Except maybe, for one thing, you and I aren't surprised by it. The shepherds had somewhere to go. They had someone to find—the baby born a King of Kings. I don't know what the journey looked like for them, but I have an idea of what it could look like for you and me. Because for you and I, our Christmas journey is the same. We turn our hearts toward heaven, and–in our souls–hear the angels declare, "Glory to God in the highest." Where do we go from there? We move toward peace.

CHALLENGE: Shout out someone in your life who did something amazing. Put it on social media, brag on them big time, or, just call them up and tell them how much what they did meant to you.

DAY 24

"But you, O Bethlehem Ephrathah, who are too little to be among the clans of Judah, from you shall come forth for me one who is to be ruler in Israel, whose coming forth is from of old, from ancient days." Micah 5:2

Have you ever forgotten something really important? We all have. It can really throw off your day when you leave your wallet or something critically important behind.

What if your entire family was forgotten? Things may have seemed that way for Bethlehem. The Prophet Micah had made a really big deal out of the role they would play in the Messiah's life. I wonder if anyone still believed it after all those years had passed? Did a group of old timers sit by the city gate every morning swapping news and guessing when their time would come? Or did they all feel forgotten?

Christmas showed them God had a plan for the little overlooked town all along. In a place that may have felt forgotten, the Savior of the world was born. God's plan of redemption was working.

Have you ever felt forgotten? Maybe you were passed over for a raise or something entirely different happened. It's not a great feeling to be ignored.

God didn't forget the role Bethlehem would play. He hasn't forgotten you, either. It may seem like it sometimes, but it isn't true.

Christmas was a new thing taking place in Bethlehem. Jesus had come. The King of Kings came home. The people long forgotten became ground zero for God's greatest plan.

Maybe you've been praying about something for a while, and it seems like God forgot you. He didn't. In fact, no matter what answer God gave you, know this. You are ground zero for the plan and the purpose He has for your life. No one else can be. It's your life. It's your purpose. And it matters to God. It matters so much Jesus came for you.

You are not forgotten. But you might be waiting. Christmas is coming.

CHALLENGE: If you find yourself in a line, a waiting room, or in some situation requiring patience, take a moment to talk to God about what you've been waiting on from Him.

DAY 25

"For to us a child is born, to us a son is given, and the government will be on his shoulders. And he will be called Wonderful Counselor, Mighty God, Everlasting Father, Prince of Peace." Isaiah 9:6 NIV

Good news is the best news. It is precisely what God promised through the Prophet Isaiah. Jesus is that promised child. He was born of a woman. He was a human man.

Jesus is the son who was given. The only begotten son of God. He was given by God—to us. Jesus is a gift. Remarkable. The Gift of God Himself born into our world to save us.

Jesus is a king. Actually, He is *the King*. That's why the prophet said the government would be upon His shoulders. Everyone will serve a king. Either you are your own king—for now. Or you serve Jesus. Here's a promise straight from scripture: One day every knee will bow to King Jesus.

Jesus represents you before God. He is our Wonderful Counselor. He advises, assists, helps, and aides. That's a pretty big deal. Don't overlook it. When was the last time you stood before God on behalf of yourself? Exactly.

Jesus is God the Son and the Son of God. He is our Mighty God. He is mighty in power, deed, love, and grace. It's precisely why He can stand before God on our behalf.

Did you know there are no orphans in Christ's kingdom? Jesus is our Everlasting Father. He is a Father to all who come to Him. FOREVER. Let that sink in.

No human can rein without the military capacity to protect his rule. Jesus is the Monarch of Mercy and crowned King of Resolution. When He whispered, "It is finished," it was done. Jesus is our Prince of Peace.

Who is Jesus to you? Trick question. He is everything Isaiah promised and more. The babe born in the manger is your good news. He is God's gift from Heaven. But none of that will make a difference in your life until you embrace the truth about Christmas. Jesus came to you so that you would come to Him.

. . .

CHALLENGE: Write a one-sentence declaration of your intention to keep moving toward God now that you've almost finished this book. To take it even further, make it the background on your smartphone.

THE DAY AFTER CHRISTMAS

Have you ever had a "Now what" moment? You waited for something—now you have it. The Children of God were waiting for the Messiah. Think about all Mary and Joseph endured. They were waiting for a Messiah. They were expecting a baby. They learned the baby would be both. They were waiting for Jesus.

Imagine how they felt after Christmas. Jesus is born! Jesus is here! Here is the Messiah! My baby! Every parent I know thinks pretty highly of their kids. Mary and Joseph actually had a reason to! But, now what? Now that we have a Savior. What do we do now? What did Mary and Joseph do?

I've really valued our time together moving closer to the heart of Christmas. As we finish up, I want to leave you with four simple things we can learn from Mary and Joseph.

HOLD JESUS CLOSE. "Mary treasured these

things in her heart." Imagine knowing the baby you hold will one day die for you. The agony of that must have been unbearable at times. What about Jesus are you holding close?

PROCLAIM JESUS. Share news about Jesus with the people close to you. Mary and Joseph didn't have to proclaim Jesus. Creation proclaimed Him. Angels proclaimed Him. The prophetess Anna proclaimed Him. "He grew in wisdom and stature with both God and men."

What do we proclaim about Jesus? His grace? His truth? His forgiveness? His healing? His coming kingdom? The best treasures are the ones we share.

MARVEL AT THE WORK OF JESUS. I love that Jesus did His very first public miracle because of His mom. She came to Him at a wedding. It makes you think there must have been some moments when Jesus did some pretty amazing things as a kid. Again and again Mary was right there. She marveled at what He did, but so did everyone else. Even His enemies marveled.

PARTICIPATE IN THE WORK OF JESUS. Joseph was going to quietly divorce Mary, until an angel told him what was going on. Jesus died for everyone, but the first people He saved were His parents. When Jesus shows up in your life salvation is the result.

The answer to "Now what" when it comes to the day after Christmas is not complicated, but it is all too often overlooked. We HOLD Jesus close. We PROCLAIM Jesus. We MARVEL at Jesus. We PARTICIPATE.

Experience what Jesus did for you. Remember, Jesus came to you so you would come to Him. Communion is all about that. It is a reminder. Jesus gave it to us as a sign. Communion is a calling card. That we belong to His family.

During communion we do three things. We look in. Doing so reminds us of the work Christ did to change our hearts. He saved us! We are not who we used to be! We look back. We take stock of how much our life has changed! We are not where we used to be! We look ahead. We know we have eternal life with Him. We can also experience a great life here and now! He wants us to live well. In faith, we believe our best days are still ahead of us. We are not where we are going to be!

CHALLENGE: Take communion with your family. I've provided a guide for how to do it below.

You will need something to represent the body and the blood of Christ. Many people prefer some kind of unleavened bread and grape juice or wine. What you use is not really that important. Why you use it and why you take communion is what truly matters. After you've gathered the supplies you need to lead your family in communion, you can continue with the script below. But this is just a guide. You may feel like you should say or do something else. Do it. The important thing here is to remember why you're doing it and to create a moment together that will challenge your heart. This is our final step together toward the heart of Christmas.

Read aloud.

"For I received from the Lord what I also delivered to you, that the Lord Jesus on the night when he was betrayed took bread, and when he had given thanks, he broke it, and said, 'This is my body which is for you. Do this in remembrance of me.' In the same way also he took the cup, after supper, saying, 'This cup is the new covenant in my blood. Do this, as often as you drink it, in remembrance of me.' For as often as you eat this bread and drink the cup, you proclaim the Lord's death until he comes. Whoever, therefore, eats the bread or drinks the cup of the Lord in an unworthy manner will be guilty concerning the body and blood of the Lord. 1 Corinthians 11: 23-27 ESV

Family Communion Guide:
The Bread

On the night when He was betrayed Jesus took the bread *(hold up your bread)* saying, "This is My body broken for you. Do this in remembrance of Me."

PRAY. Use your own words to thank Jesus for giving His body to be broken for us. Eat the bread.

. . .

The Cup

Then Jesus took the cup *(hold up your cup)* saying, "This is My blood poured out for the forgiveness of sins. Do this in remembrance of Me."

PRAY. Use your own words to thank Jesus for saving you from your sins. Drink your cup.

Family Chat

What did you learn about Christmas this week?

Have you made Christ the King of your heart?

Which challenge was the hardest? Which one was easy?

How is God drawing you closer to Him right now?

Where did you need help from someone?

Where did you help someone else?

Do you feel like Christmas means more to you today? How?

What are you looking forward to most this Christmas?

CHRISTMAS JOURNAL

_____

_____

_____

_____

_____

_____

_____

_____

_____

_____

BONUS CHAPTER

The following is a work in progress excerpt from "Everyday Jesus" coming Summer 2023.

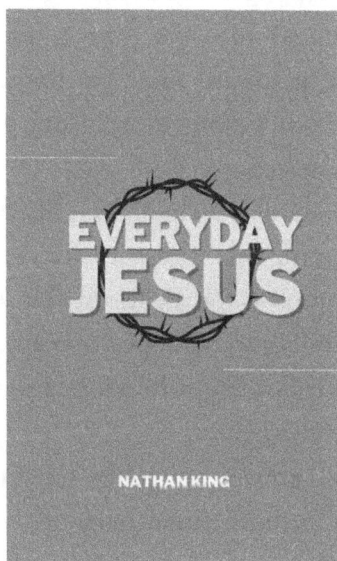

"I need help," the young soldier told me with tears in his eyes. "Can you help me?" The tears continued to roll down his face as we stood in the lobby of the church hundreds of people streaming past us on their way to lunch.

The brilliant capable young man stood before me in anguish. Who could say no to someone in such turmoil? "I can help you." I promised him.

I prayed for him right where we stood. We exchanged phone numbers and I promised to meet up with him later that week. So when Friday morning rolled around we were sitting across from each other in an old train car downtown that doubles as a cafe.

Roger began to open up to me about all of his recent struggles. He had left a trail of broken relationships and bad habits behind him. He had a tide of uncertain outcomes rolling toward him. He found himself at a crossroads and was looking for someone who could help him take his next step.

We talked about his childhood. He had two loving parents who were still together after many years. We talked about his plans for the future. He was excelling in his role in the military and hoped to make a career out of it. And, as we talked about his faith the crux of Roger's struggles came into light.

Roger had grown up going to church with his parents. That is, until some religious whack jobs did some really stupid stuff leaving his dad fed up and frustrated with church. Roger's dad never looked back. He left church behind. He left Jesus behind. And he left his young son behind just as he was trying to find out what role Jesus was going to have in his life.

The spiritual abandonment left Roger wandering during his formative years. When he was trying to look to his father for help—his dad had hung a "closed" sign on the door to his heart. That would be hard for anyone, but it's especially hard for a young man with a strong sense of justice. One hoping for a hand from the most important man in his life.

Once his dad checked out, Roger's life went into a tailspin of bad habits. His everyday life became a reflection of his father's struggle. Roger believed deeply in Jesus. He believed Jesus was the Son of God. But he didn't know what that was supposed to mean for his everyday life.

Roger didn't know how or even if Jesus fit into his relationships. He didn't know how much Jesus wanted to be part of his future plans. He didn't understand how much Jesus valued and treasured the man he was becoming. He didn't know where to turn to find the answers his young heart was yearning for.

In his heart he wanted to believe. He desperately wanted it. He had been holding on to hope.

His story laid out before me Roger sighed. "See how messed up I am?" I gave him my best smile. I was full of so much hope for him. But I knew what I wanted for Roger was only a drop in the bucket compared to what Jesus wanted him to realize.

So I made Roger a promise. It's the same promise I've lived by for years now. It's the promise that changed my life more than thirty years ago. It's the promise I've tried to help people understand for the last twenty five years. It's the best promise anyone can know who is struggling to find their footing when it comes to faith, habits, choices, relationships, and so many of life's opportunities.

"Everyday with Jesus is better than any day without him."

WHAT JESUS WANTS

Way too many people are living a life far too much like the one Roger struggled with. Until he realized that Jesus is an Everyday Jesus. Until he realized Jesus wanted to be part of his everyday life. Jesus wants the same thing for you.

So many people are living life without Jesus. Maybe they go to church on Sunday in order to check some kind of religious, cultural, or familial obligation off their list. Most don't even do that. Most people just ignore Jesus altogether.

How does Jesus influence your daily life? If you are living without him you are missing what he wants for you. In fact, he died so your life could be different.

Perhaps the reality of your present situation is that your life is not influenced by Jesus. You go to work without him. You navigate your home life and essential relationships without him. Even your habits and hobbies are missing what he wants for you.

The simple truth is that Jesus loves you. A life lived without him is much less than what it could be. If that's you—you're right where Roger was. You need to embrace the same promise Roger came to realize. Jesus is an Everyday Jesus. Everyday with Jesus is better than any day without him.

When you do you will treat the people around you differently. Your relationships will become better than you ever dreamed they could be. When Jesus becomes part of your everyday reality you will treat yourself differently too. Your personal habits will shift. Your emotional well-being will become better. You will find peace and joy inside. Your strength to face your struggles will come from someone who wants nothing but the best for you.

Living everyday with Jesus shouldn't be complicated —it should be simple and straightforward. Life with Jesus should be personal. Life with Jesus should be full of grace. Life with Jesus should be full of purpose.

If you have found yourself struggling with any of those things it's time to disrupt the status quo. It's time to walk away from where you've been. It's time to move into the kind of life Jesus has always wanted for you. One where he is. It's time to embrace Jesus everyday.

That's what this book is about. I want to help you realize how simple life with Jesus is. I want you to know how much freedom there is. I hope you will come away full of hope. I want your heart to fill up on the kind of hope Jesus has for you. I want you to realize what it looks like when grace is part of your everyday rhythm. I want you to find purpose. One that surges inside you daily as you walk hand in hand with Jesus—everyday.

You'll learn what Roger, myself, and countless others have discovered across the ages: Everyday with Jesus is better than any day without him.

Enjoy "The Christmas Trail Guide"?

Check out these resources.

SUBSCRIBE FOR DEVOS THAT MATTER. 60 SECONDS OR LESS. EVERY WEEKDAY.

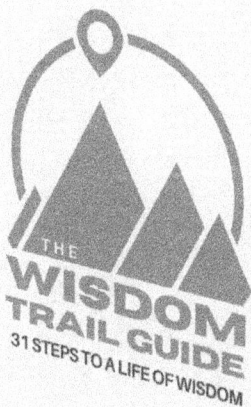

The Wisdom Trail Guide: 31 Steps to a Life of Wisdom

Paperback & eBook – July 2021

by Nathan King

"Wisdom is not something God wants *from* you. It's something God wants *for* you."

Wisdom is not something reserved for a select few. Wisdom is not meant to be hidden away from you. Wisdom is available to everyone. God wants you to experience a life of Wisdom. Nathan King has been helping others take their next step toward the life of Wisdom God wants for them for two decades.

"The Wisdom Trail Guide: 31 Steps to a Life of Wisdom" offers insight from 31 daily entries in the Book of Proverbs. Each entry offers practical insight coupled with real life situations anyone searching for Wisdom can relate to.

"The Wisdom Trail Guide" is formatted to be a quick and easy read. One that doesn't consume a lot of your time; but offers a thoughtful response for each day. Read it on your own, with a friend, or in a group. The challenges and prayers included inside will help you take your next step forward.

In *"The Wisdom Trail Guide"* pastor and adjunct professor Nathan King lays out 31 clear steps anyone can take. Steps that can reshape how you see yourself, how you interact with the people around you, and how you approach your life.

Fear, forgiveness, decision making, friends, work, family and more are tackled during the four week journey that will challenge and encourage the life of anyone looking to take their next step toward a life of Wisdom.

NATHAN KING

LEARN
LOVE
LIVE

THE STORY GOD WANTS
FOR YOUR LIFE

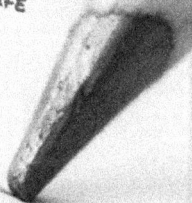

Learn Love Live: The Story God Wants for Your Life

Paperback & eBook – January 2022

by Nathan King

What if YOU could live a better story?

You have a story. It is the story of the life you are living, the ones you love, and the way God is helping you learn to follow Him. Your story is incredible, because it is yours. I know this because I have lived it. Living through each of these things has taught me the power of the love God has for us. It has shown me just how amazing life becomes when we begin to love the people around us in amazing ways. The way God wants us to. So, what does God want for you? Easy. He wants you to ...

LEARN. LOVE. LIVE.

The Story God Wants for Your Life

About The Author

Nathan King lives with his family in Arkansas. You can often find him riding his bike off the side of a mountain, building something with his hands, or catching the latest superhero movie with his family. He and Jamie have the distinct privilege of serving as pastors at New Life Church in Conway, AR. You can find him online at www.nathanking.com, YouTube.com/@TheBibleShorts, tiktok.com/@nathanking.com, or in his neighborhood walking his dog. For speaking inquiries contact help@nathanking.com.

9 781737 469162